101 Systems Theory Quotes

One Hundred and One Quotes on
BFST for the Novice and
the Curious

Israel Galindo

101 Systems Theory Quotes: One Hundred and One Quotes on BFST for the Novice and the Curious

Cover by Israel Galindo

Published by Didache Press

CONTENTS

Introduction

Bowen Family Systems Theory has become a significant resource for many clergy and congregational leaders. Since the groundbreaking volume by Edwin H. Friedman in 1985, *Generation to Generation,* the theory continues to be an influential "theory of practice" for ministry. As a *bona fide* theory, that is, one grounded in a field of study and practice, BFST provides a more rigorous framework as a theory of practice than devotional, romantic, metaphoric, or individualistic understandings of the role of clergy in a particular context, the congregation.

Murray Bowen developed BFST, or "Bowen Theory," from the clinical therapeutic context. The theory provides a framework for interpreting the emotional process of relationships as they are manifested in the context (the "emotional field") of a particular family constellation. The theory has been applied to other relationship systems beyond the biological family unit, including institutions, government, social networks, and for over twenty years, congregations. Bowen and Kerr identified eight interlocking components which comprises BFST. The eight concepts are:

1. Triangles

2. Differentiation of Self

3. Nuclear Family Emotional System

4. Family Projection Process

5. Multigenerational Transmission Process

6. Emotional Cutoff

7. Sibling Position

8. Societal Emotional Process.

Within those eight integrated concepts lies a framework that can describe and interpret the complex interactions of individuals in relationship systems. Each concept can, to some extent, provide a way to approach the question of pastoral leadership from the perspective of the interaction between the functioning of clergy and the congregational context in which the relationship between church and pastor finds expression, or, the function of leaders in organizations.

For pastoral leaders, BFST can inform three main therapeutic interventions for ministry contexts: (1) working to understand one's family of origin to gain insight on one's formation of self and of how one functions in relationships; (2) committing to the ongoing work of differentiation of self—working on one's maturity, being one's own self in the midst of relationships, clarifying one's principles and values, working on functioning non-anxiously during times of high reactivity, and staying emotionally connected and present in key relationships, and, (3) managing anxious relationships by functioning better in triangles.

Emotional Process

"The emotional system is the force that motivates; the relationship system is the way it is expressed."

Murray Bowen, *Family Therapy in Clinical Practice*

"A problem common to all systems theory: how to account for change at all if systems are perpetually kept in balance by their own homeostatic forces."

Edwin H. Friedman, *A Failure of Nerve*

✳ "Institutions are emotional fields that generally affect the functioning of their members more than the members affect the field."

Edwin H. Friedman, *Generation to Generation*

"Operationally I regard the emotional system as something deep that is in contact with cellular and somatic processes, and a feeling system as bridge that is in contact with parts of the emotional system on one side and with the intellectual system on the other."

Murray Bowen, *Family Therapy in Clinical Practice*

"Distinguishing facts and functional facts from nonfacts is a *sine qua non* or accurate observation of emotional process in human relationship systems, whether the context is one of research or the psychoanalytic or some other significant relationship."

Patricia A. Comella, "Observing Emotional Functioning in Human Relationship Systems"

"Homeostasis refers to the "balance" a system achieves to help maintain the emotional process patterns that help ensure its functional perception of viability (though not necessarily its vitality), identity, and functioning. The concept is not "static"—it is a dynamic. As congregations adapt to changing environments and to the arc of its lifespan, sometimes including traumas, resilient congregations are able to modify or modulate homeostasis. This requires adaptation not only of the congregation, but of a long-term pastor who can accept that change is the norm over the course of a long ministry, and that real leadership is the capacity to manage the anxiety about the change."

Israel Galindo and Betty Pugh Mills, "Long-term Pastorates and Bowen Family Systems Theory"

"The extent we function and grow within the context of our own souls (a lifetime project) and abet the emergence of our own selves (by a willingness to face life's challenges and oneself), our spirituality and our tradition will spring naturally from our being."

Edwin H. Friedman, *Generation to Generation*

"Within the family emotional system, the emotional tensions shift about in an orderly series of emotional alliances and rejection."

Murray Bowen

"Chronic illness is an adaptation to a relationship."

Edwin H. Friedman, *A Failure of Nerve*

"Any time one key member of an organization can be responsibly responsible for self, the problem in an organization will resolve."

Murray Bowen, *Family Therapy in Clinical Practice*

"For the purpose of this theoretical-therapeutic system, I think of the family as a combination of 'emotional' and 'relationship' systems. The term *emotional* refers to the force that motivates the system and *relationship* to the ways it is expressed. Under relationship would be subsumed communication, interaction, and other relationship modalities."

Murray Bowen, *Family Therapy in Clinical Practice*

"I've used the term emotion as synonymous with *instinct*—and an instinct is a biological phenomenon which takes place automatically in the organism.

Murray Bowen in "Various Theoretical Points People Miss," Mary Bourne (ed)

"The concept of the motional system makes a distinction between emotion and feelings. Emotional process is considered synonymous with instinctual process, while feelings reflect the more superficial aspects of emotional functioning. This means that the feeling process is linked to the more basic emotional process.

The way people mange feelings is a reflection of forces operating in the emotionally governed relationship system. People are programmed to manage feelings in certain ways based on these forces."

Murray Bowen in "An Obstacle to 'Hearing' Bowen Theory ,"Mary Bourne (ed)

"It has been my impression that at any gathering, whether it be public or private, those who are quickest to inject words like sensitivity, empathy, consensus, trust, confidentiality, and togetherness into their arguments have perverted these humanitarian words into power tools to get others to adapt to them."

Edwin H. Friedman, *A Failure of Nerve*

"Human beings have an intense need for emotional closeness, but are also allergic to too much of it."

Murray Bowen, *Family Therapy in Clinical Practice*

"Emotional process occurs automatically in a relationship context and involves the reciprocal responding of living organisms to each other and to the conditions of life to which they must adapt to survive or enjoy an acceptable level of well-being. Emotional process includes appraisals of those relationships and conditions of life and the internal sates generated by such appraisals; it is seen in nonhuman species as well as in the human species. It appears to be a defining characteristic of life on Earth and is essential to survival and well-being at both the individual and group levels.

. . .

"Emotional process regulates, and at times may govern, behavior and functioning, especially during times of imminent or potential threat to survival or well-being."

Patricia A. Comella, "Observing Emotional Functioning in Human Relationship Systems"

"The focus on "need fulfillment" that so often accompanies an emphasis on empathy leaves out the possibility that what another may really "need" (to become more responsible) is *not* to have their needs fulfilled. Indeed, it is not even clear that feeling for others is a more caring stance (or even a more ethical stance) than challenging than to take responsibility for themselves."

Edwin H. Friedman, *A Failure of Nerve*

"The one who functions for long periods in the adaptive position gradually loses the ability to function and make decisions for self. At that point, it requires no more than a moderate increase in stress to trigger the adaptive one into dysfunction, which can be physical illness, emotional illness, or social illness, such as drinking, acting out, and irresponsible behavior."

Murray Bowen, *Family Therapy in Clinical Practice*

"Physiological, social, and ecological processes all operate simultaneously and none is more important or fundamental than another. Linking levels of organization is central to any study of social behavior. For humans and social animals, an individual's behavior is always embedded in a social world."

Deborah M. Gordon, *Ants at Work*

"The functioning of individuals in any institution is not determined by their nature (personality) but by their position within a relationship system, as well as by what other "cells" will permit them to do."

Edwin H. Friedman, *A Failure of Nerve*

"For an individual to move beyond being sensitive to others toward an explicit other-orientation requires a shift in perspective. The emotional state induced in oneself by the other now needs to be attributed to the other instead of the self. A heightened self-identity allows a subject to relate to the object's emotional state without losing sight of the actual source of this state."

Frans de Waal, "Putting the Altruism Back into Altruism: The Evolution of Empathy"

Differentiation of Self

"The theory postulates two opposing basic life forces. One is a built-in life growth force toward individuality and the differentiation of a separate 'self,' and the other an equally intense emotional closeness."

Murray Bowen, *Family Therapy in Clinical Practice*

"All things being equal, most people will live the characteristics they developed in their families of origin. It is an unusual person that changes that."

Mary Bourne (ed),"Various Theoretical Points People Miss"

"The concept of differentiation of self speaks to issues of identity, leadership, and the pastor's role and function in the clergy-congregation relationship. Defined simply, differentiation of self is the capacity of the individual to cope with circumstances, relationships, and life in general within a relative scale of functioning, with adaptation and resilience being two key qualities.

"... differentiation of self mediates a person's capacity to avoid fusion with others in the system, to function better in the midst of acute anxiety in times of crises. Differentiation of self refers to the extent a person can think and act maturely and principled while in the midst of emotionally charged issues (a situation all too common, and frequent, for clergy). It is the capacity to be yourself while at the same time, remaining emotionally and mindfully connected to others, even in highly stressful circumstances. The concept of differentiation of self proposes that a highly functioning and mature person has the capacity to discern the difference between the experiences of thoughts and feelings, can manage their own reactivity better, and is able to choose thoughtful, principled actions even in the midst of reactivity."

Israel Galindo and Betty Pugh Mills, "Long-tenured Ministry and Systems Theory"

"It is possible for [persons] to discriminate between emotions and the intellect and to slowly gain more conscious control over emotional functioning. There are definite characteristics of those who can do this more readily and those who are a few years slower. The name of that is differentiation of self."

Murray Bowen, *Family Therapy in Clinical Context*

"In the context of intense relationships, like a family or a congregation, differentiation of self mediates a person's capacity to avoid fusion with others in the system, to function better in the midst of acute anxiety in times of crises. Differentiation of self refers to the extent a person can think and act maturely and principled while in the midst of emotionally charged issues (a situation all too common, and frequent, for clergy). It is the capacity to be yourself while at the same time, remaining emotionally and mindfully connected to others, even in highly stressful circumstances. The concept of differentiation of self proposes that a highly functioning and mature person has the capacity to discern the difference between the experiences of thoughts and feelings, can manage their own reactivity better, and is able to choose thoughtful, principled actions even in the midst of reactivity."

Israel Galindo and Betty Pugh Mills, "Long-tenured Ministry and Systems Theory: Bowen Systems Theory As A Resource for the Long Haul"

"I consider rugged individualism to be an exaggerated present posture of a person struggling against emotional fusion. The differentiated person is always aware of others and the relationship system around him."

Murray Bowen, *Family Therapy in Clinical Practice*

"Anyone who wishes to advance our species or an institution must possess those qualities which those who have little sense of self will perceive as narcissistic. All this besides the fact that "arrogant," "headstrong," "narcissistic," and "cold" will be the terms used against any person who tries to be more himself or herself."

Edwin H. Friedman, *A Failure of Nerve*

Individuals at higher levels of differentiation "have enough confidence in their ability to deal with relationships, even emotionally intense ones, so that they neither avoid them nor become highly anxious in encountering them."

Kerr and Bowen, *Family Evaluation*

"If differentiation is an effort to be successful, it has to take place in action, as a result of careful private planning, and without previous announcement of one's plan."

Murray Bowen, *Family Therapy in Clinical Practice*

"The process [of differentiation of self] includes experiences that promote new learning: becoming a better observer of reactivity in self and in the family system; containing and managing one's own reactivity; defining operating principles for self in every area of life; acting on principles in the face of automatic reactions; and working to become more objective and thoughtful in relation to others and more responsible in one's own life. Steps toward differentiation include making and maintaining contact with every living family member, increasing factual knowledge about one's family and family history, being present at intense and anxious times in the family, and actively interacting with family to develop relationships in which thinking is engaged."

Murray Bowen, *Family Therapy in Clinical Practice*

"The greater the fusion between emotion and intellect,
the more the individual is fused into the emotional
fusions of people around him ... It is possible for man to
discriminate between the emotions and the intellect
and to slowly gain more conscious control
of emotional functioning."

Murray Bowen, *Family Therapy in Clinical Practice*

"Differentiation of self occurs on a continuum. In Bowen theory, differentiation refers both to the degree of fusion between intellectual and emotional functioning in an individual and the degree to which one self fuses or merges into another self in a close emotional relationship. According to Bowen theory, these two broad definitions of differentiation intertwine. The greater the relative differentiation between intellectual and emotional functioning in a family member, the more that person is able to maintain a greater degree of differentiation in relationship with other members in the family."

Randall T. Frost, "Challenges of Conducting Research"

"People with the most fusion have most of the human problems, and those with the most differentiation, the fewest; but there can be people with intense fusion who manage to keep their relationships in balance, who are never subjected to severe stress, who never develop symptoms and who appear normal. However their life adjustments are tenuous, and, if they are stressed into dysfunction, the impairment can be chronic or permanent. There are also fairly well-differentiated people who can be stressed into dysfunction, but they recover rapidly."

Murray Bowen, *Family Therapy in Clinical Practice*

"People above 50 [on the Scale of Differentiation] have developed a reasonable level of solid self on most of the essential issues in life. In periods of calm, they have employed logical reasoning to develop beliefs, principles, and convictions that they use to overrule the emotional system in situations of anxiety and panic."

Murray Bowen, *Family Therapy in Clinical Practice*

"There is a tilt toward the togetherness end of the scale, however, when a relationship system becomes emotionally regressed.

"The way out of [the] dilemma is not finding the proper balance of self and togetherness, but by reorienting one's understanding of togetherness and self so that they are made continuous rather than polarized."

Edwin H. Friedman, *A Failure of Nerve*

"Self differentiation is . . . a force that is not anti-togetherness; on the contrary, it is a force that modifies the emotional processes within any group's togetherness so that a leader actually promotes community through the emerging self-differentiation (autonomy, independence, individuality) of the other members."

Edwin H. Friedman, *A Failure of Nerve*

"Success in achieving differentiation of self can be measured, I believe, in the extent to which one can be a part of the family without automatically being one of the "emotional dominoes." The path towards such a goal can be achieved best not by a process of internal analysis of oneself but through a process of eternal perceptions that analyze the system. In other words, I do not thing in terms of a *sense* of self, which seems too unverifiable, but in terms of a *position* of self."

Edwin H. Friedman, "The Birthday Party Revisited: Family Therapy and the Problem of Change" in *The Therapist's Own Family*

"When the intellectual system has the option to operate independently of the feeling system, it is possible for an individual to do for himself without being selfish and to so for others without being selfless. This becomes possible when behavior is based more on principle than on the obligatory pressure of the feeling system."

Murray Bowen, *Family Therapy in Clinical Practice*

"One test of differentiation is the ability of a person to take a more principled position and hold it against the opposition of important others."

Murray Bowen, *Family Therapy in Clinical Practice*

Triangles

"We live our lives in networks of emotional forces that follow triangle patterns."

Murray Bowen

"A two-person system is inherently unstable. Triangles are the smallest stable relationship system, the molecules of an emotional system."

Murray Bowen

"Emotional triangles outlast people. They are passed on as legacies from generation to generation. Even though differentiation is never finished, each slight modification—each increment of change—broadens a vision once limited by family processes that long ago had ceased to be useful."

Susan S. Edwards, "Defining Self After the Last Child Leaves Home" in *The Therapist's Own Family.*

"The triangle, a three-party relationship system, is the smallest emotionally stable relationship system in which anxiety at a given level of intensity can be confined to the threesome. Within a triangle, the mechanism for managing the stresses in the relationships among the three are entirely predictable. Should the intensity increase beyond what the threesome can manage, they will predictably "triangle" in another party and, if necessary, others, until the triangles and interlocking triangles defining the relationship system contain the anxiety. . . . Through triangles and interlocking triangles, anxiety may be transmitted from one relationship system to another."

Patricia A. Comella, "Observing Emotional Functioning in Human Relationship Systems"

"In complex relationship systems, like congregations, triangles can become part of the structure of the system, at which point several interlocking triangles help distribute anxiety and create patterns of relationships. As with all concepts in BFST, triangles are neither "good" not "bad." They are merely a natural functional dynamic in any relationship system. Persons who become part of a dynamic anxiety triangle may function in it to the extent they have capacity to differentiate within its structure—remaining neutral but connected, or becoming part of the reactivity that drives the triangled relationship. Understanding one's position in the triangle is paramount to one's leadership function."

Israel Galindo and Betty Pugh Mills, "Long-term Pastorates and Bowen Family Systems Theory"

"If a person is able to modify his or her part in a key fixed triangle in specifiable ways, then the emotional system becomes more flexible, less stuck together and the family is better able to adapt to stress."

Randall T. Frost, "The Predictability of the Family Emotional System"

"The popular belief is that one can remove one's self from triangles at will and that work on internal symptoms is more productive than the modification of triangles in which [one] has been involved for many years. What most people do not know, is that vulnerability to symptoms is directly proportional to participation in emotional triangles, which restrict the capacity for the differentiation of self."

Susan S. Edwards, "Defining Self After the Last Child Leaves Home" in *The Therapist's Own Family.*

"... it is possible to see the triangles in which one grew up, and to be different in relation to them. The process of detriangling is essentially the same as has been described in doing family therapy with two spouses. . . . The overall goal is to be constantly in contact with an emotional issue involving two other people and self, without taking sides, without counterattacking or defending self, and to always have a neutral response."

Murray Bowen, *Family Therapy in Clinical Practice*

"It is a clinical fact that the original two-person tension system will resolve itself automatically when contained within a three-person system, one of whom remains emotionally detached."

Murray Bowen

"It is promoting responsibility for self in another through challenge [that is caring and self-preserving]. But that requires raising one's own threshold for their pain and not being sensitive to their sensitivities."

Edwin H. Friedman, *A Failure of Nerve*

Leadership

"'No good deed goes unpunished'; chronic criticism is, if anything, often a sign that the leader is functioning better! Vision is not enough."

Edwin H. Friedman, *A Failure of Nerve*

"The influencing potential of the nonanxious presence is not to be confused with being "cool" or being "nice." Nor is it to be construed as denying anxiety in ourselves, as if unaffected by events. The nonanxious presence involves engagement, being there and taking the heat if need be, witnessing the pain, and yet not fighting fire with fire. The nonanxious presence means we are aware of our own anxiety and the anxiety of others, but we will not let wither determine our actions. Obviously this means that we have some capacity to tolerate pain both in ourselves and in others."

Peter L. Steinke, *Congregational Leadership in Anxious Times*

"Leadership is essentially an emotional process rather than a cognitive phenomenon."

Edwin H. Friedman, *A Failure of Nerve*

"The position most dangerous to a leader's health is what I call the 'togetherness position,' in which the leader feels responsible for keeping a system together."

Edwin H. Friedman, *A Failure of Nerve*

"… leadership in the congregational context is primarily a corporate function, not an individual one. It has more to do with the leader's function in the system than it does with the leader's personality or even with the ability to motivate others."

Israel Galindo, *The Hidden Lives of Congregations*

"It may be said unequivocally that whenever anyone is *in extremis* (whether it is a marital crisis, an economic crisis, a political crisis, or a health crisis), their chances of survival are far greater when their horizons are formed of projected images from their own imagination rather than being limited by what they can actually see."

Edwin H. Friedman, *A Failure of Nerve*

"The great lesson here for all imaginatively gridlocked systems is that the acceptance and even cherishing of uncertainty is critical to keeping the human mind from voyaging into the delusion of omniscience."

Edwin H. Friedman, *A Failure of Nerve*

"The critical importance of leadership for the health of an organization justifies the action of members of any institution to replace poorly defined leaders."

Edwin H. Friedman, *A Failure of Nerve*

"Leadership through self-differentiation is not easy;
learning techniques and imbibing data are far easier.
Nor is striving or achieving success as a leader without
pain: there is the pain of isolation, the pain of loneliness,
the pain of personal attacks, the pain of losing friends.
That's what leadership is all about."

Edwin H. Friedman, *A Failure of Nerve*

"The leader is in a position to influence the emotional
field. The leader's positive influence is most dramatic at
times of crisis, bewilderment, stagnancy, and new
situations. . . . The leader's positive influence in crucial
times is accomplished through both the leader's being
(demeanor, spirit, and poise) as well as the leader's
thoughtful functioning. Both attitude and action
influence outcomes."

Peter L. Steinke, *Congregational Leadership in
Anxious Times*

"Despite its anxiety-provoking effects, the proliferation of data also has an addictive quality. Leaders, healers, and parents "imbibe" data as a way of dealing with their own chronic anxiety. The pursuit of data, in almost any field, has come to resemble a form of substance abuse, accompanied by all the usual problems of addiction: self-doubt, denial, temptation, relapse, and withdrawal. Leadership training programs thus wind up in the codependent position of enablers, with publishers often in the role of "suppliers." What does it take to get parents, healers, and managers, when they hear of the latest quick-fix fad that has just been published, to "just say no"?"

Edwin H. Friedman, *A Failure of Nerve*

"A willingness to be exposed and vulnerable. One of the major limitations of imagination's fruits is the fear of standing out. It is more than a fear of criticism. It is anxiety at being alone, of being in a position where one can rely little on others, a position that puts one's own resources to the test, a position where one will have to take total responsibility for one's own response to the environment. Leaders must not only not be afraid of that position; they must come to love it."

Edwin H. Friedman, *A Failure of Nerve*

"One of the most important leadership functions that congregational leaders must provide during times of change is that of staying connected. This is especially true when change challenges the homeostasis of the congregation and brings the hidden life force of Systemic Anxiety to the forefront. The tendency of most leaders seems to be to hunker down and fly under the radar—hoping to become a less visible target for the more vocal and resistant members in the congregation. This is unfortunate, because what is most needed at those times is for the leader to stay connected to those very persons."

Israel Galindo, *The Hidden Lives of Congregations*

"The colossal misunderstanding of our time is the assumption that insight will work with people who are unmotivated to change. Communication does not depend on syntax, or eloquence, or rhetoric, or articulation but on the emotional context in which the message is being heard. People can only hear you when they are moving toward you, and they are not likely to when your words are pursuing them. Even the choices words lose their power when they are used to overpower. Attitudes are the real figures of speech."

Edwin H. Friedman, *A Failure of Nerve*

"The understanding that one can get more change in a family or organization by working with the motivated members (the strengths) in the system than by focusing on the symptomatic or recalcitrant members totally obliterates the search for answers to the question of how to motivate the unmotivated."

Edwin H. Friedman, *A Failure of Nerve*

"Living with crisis is a major part of leaders' lives. The crises come in two major varieties: (1) those that are not of their making but are imposed on them from outside or within the system; and (2) those that are actually triggered by the leaders through doing precisely what they should be doing."

Edwin H. Friedman, *A Failure of Nerve*

"Leaders must not only develop vision, persistence, and stamina, but also understand that the problems they encounter may stem from their own unresolved family issues. . . ."

Edwin H. Friedman, *A Failure of Nerve*

Anxiety and Reactivity

"While not one of the eight foundational concepts, anxiety is a key concept in BFST that helps describe, and interpret, emotional process dynamics in a relationship system. In the theory anxiety is a natural part of any biological system and network of relationships, from families to organizations. The theory distinguishes between acute and chronic anxiety and how they can manifest in reactivity behaviors like sabotage, herding, misdirected attack, and group-think."

Israel Galindo and Betty Pugh Mills, "Long-tenured Ministry and Systems Theory"

"Anxiety along will not harm or endanger a system. How anxiety is addressed will determine outcome more than anything."

Peter L. Steinke, *Congregational Leadership in Anxious Times*

"But what is clear about pain universally is this: To the extent that we are motivated to get on with life, we seem to be able to tolerate more pain; in other words, our threshold seems to increase. Conversely, to the extent that we are unmotivated to get out of our chair, our threshold seems to go down."

Edwin H. Friedman, *A Failure of Nerve*

"All pathogenic lack self-regulation and therefore (a) are invasive by nature and (b) cannot be expected to learn from their experience."

Murray Bowen, *Family Therapy in Clinical Practice*

"...sustained chronic anxiety is a necessary condition for a societal regression, which is a process that over time compromises a society's capacity for making intellectually determined choices. Choices increasingly become emotionally driven to allay the sustained chronic anxiety. The anxiety is an automatic, instinctual response to a sustained, underlying threat that is unknown, unacknowledged, unrecognized, or all of these at a social level."

Patricia A. Comella, "Observing Emotional Functioning in Human Relationship Systems"

"Anxiety is the automatic and natural reaction to anything that might threaten a person's safety. As anxiety increases in emotional systems, people's behavior is more automatic. That means people are less thoughtful and imaginative, resistant to whatever signals pain, and generally in an edgy mood."

Peter L. Steinke, *Congregational Leadership in Anxious Times*

"According to Bowen systems theory, Systemic Anxiety tends to seek out and settle on three predictable places: the most dependent in the system, the most vulnerable in the system, and in the most responsible in the system, the leader. The "reason" an anxious system in crisis focuses on the least-differentiated or most dependent in the system is to cause the leadership position to respond to the acting out (the symptomology) so that the system can get back to a more comfortable homeostasis. That is, when the persons in the leadership position defect in place or underfunction—and thereby do not provide the system with the leadership functions it needs—the hidden life force of Systemic Anxiety will come to rest on predictable systemic positions (on the most vulnerable or the ones with the least capacity to tolerate anxiety or change) in order to create sufficient symptomology to cause the person(s) in the leadership position to get back on the ball and do what he or she is supposed to do for the system: to help regulate it."

Israel Galindo, *The Hidden Lives of Congregations*

"If people are successful in modifying the degree of emotional cut off with their family of origin, then anxiety will come down in the nuclear family which in turn will also attenuate the severity of symptoms in the nuclear family. . . ."

Randall T. Frost, "The Predictability of the Family Emotional System"

"The fact that chronically anxious families will always lack well-differentiated leadership is absolutely universal."

Edwin H. Friedman, *A Failure of Nerve*

"People's flexibility to adapt is directly related to their level of chronic anxiety and the relationship systems to which they belong."

Patricia A. Comella, "Observing Emotional Functioning in Human Relationship Systems"

"A major criterion for judging the anxiety level of any society is the loss of its capacity to be playful."

Edwin H. Friedman, *A Failure of Nerve*

"The amount of chronic anxiety in a [system] is inversely proportional to its capacity for ensuring pain."

Edwin H. Friedman, *A Failure of Nerve*

"Reactivity ... eventually makes chronically anxious families leaderless, either because it prevents potential leaders from emerging in the first place or because it wears leaders down by sabotaging their initiatives and resolve with constant automatic responses."

Edwin H. Friedman, *A Failure of Nerve*

"Should internal or external stresses increase to the level of anxiety in the emotional unit such that the anxiety can no longer be contained in the system, the excess anxiety will be projected externally through triangles and interlocking triangles, thereby redefining the emotional unit. To accurately observe functioning within an emotional unit, one must be able to describe the external environment within which the emotional unit is functioning, understand functioning within the unit, and understand how the . . . unit and external environment interrelate and mutually influence each other."

Patricia A. Comella, "Observing Emotional Functioning in Human Relationship Systems"

"The life pattern of cutoffs is determined by the way people handle their unresolved emotional attachments to their parents. . . . The concept deals with the way people separate themselves from the past in order to start their lives in the present generation.

The therapeutic effort is to convert the cutoff into an orderly differentiation of a self from the extended family."

Murray Bowen, *Family Therapy in Clinical Practice*

"In an emotional cutoff, it is not possible to cut onself off from the chronic anxiety that has been transmitted multigenerationally through the projection process in each generation. However, there is cutoff from knowledge of the courses of the anxiety which makes it more likely that efforts to transcend the anxiety will prove ineffective. The chronic anxiety will continue to have constraing effect on functioning.

Patricia A. Comella, "Observing Emotional Functioning in Human Relationship Systems"

"There is correlation between emotional cutoff in the family and the emotional blindness that impinges on perception and experience. In a general sense, the more emotional cutoff from the family, the more intense the feeling states, and the more polarized the perspective on emotional relationship."

Priscilla J. Friesen, in "A Systems View of the Training Program at the Bowen Center"

"The task of exploring and reinterpreting a cut-off requires three fundamental shifts in perspective: (1) from a predominantly instinctive or emotional response to a predominantly cognitive, rational position; (2) from cause-and-effect to process thinking; and (3) from considering the self as the focus of attention to seeing the family or the system as the context of experience. These are radical changes in perspective."

Ellen G. Benswanger, "Strategies to Explore Cut-Offs" in *The Therapist's Own Family*

"Cutting off a relationship by physical or emotional distance does not end the emotional process; in fact it intensifies it. If one cuts off his relationship with his parents or siblings, the emotional sensitivities and yearnings from these relationships tend to push into new relationships, with a spouse or with children, seeking all the more urgently for resolution. The new relationships will tend to become problematic under this pressure and lead to further distancing and cut-offs."

Carter, E. A. and Orfandis, M. M., "Family Therapy With One Person and the Family Therapist's Own Family," in *Family Therapy.*

"At times of crisis, a congregation functions best when its key leaders are differentiated. The crisis certainly ushers in confusion, despair, and a temporary period of powerlessness and hopelessness. It is a crucial time for the community to slow down and to reflect on what happened. The natural instinct is just the opposite—to press immediately for decisions, explanations, and actions to dispel the awful uncertainty and helplessness. Impatience has its source in anxiety. Experience has taught us that healing has its own timetable. Being hasty is low-road functioning."

Peter L. Steinke, *Congregational Leadership in Anxious Times*

Family of Origin
and Parenting

"(Maternal anxiety may be the original addiction.) To some extent, the child's reaction will depend on the extent to which mother used the child as her own addiction, fusing with the child to ward off rejection or pain in her own life. The withdrawal phenomenon in a child is more severe to the extent that the child was originally mother's analgesic. Either way, the intensity of the symptom that surfaces will be proportional to the amount of pain the child was originally spared. This need for a "fix" can occur in any relationship, however, even between a shepherd and his flock."

Edwin H. Friedman, *Generation to Generation*

"In general, I would say when a symptom focuses in a young child that would be by now the entire family has the notion that they problem is in the child. So another way of thinking, or a way of thinking . . . if you're thinking systems the basic problem is in all the people around that child."

Murray Bowen in "Various Theoretical Points People Miss," Mary Bourne (ed)

"Perhaps one of the most "mystical" of the eight concepts is that of the multigenerational transmission of emotional process in biological families. This concept describes how patterns of emotional process are passed down generation to generation in family systems. The same phenomenon can be seen in congregations. The concept offers a way of understanding how relationship patterns in a congregation go beyond the personality and individual qualities of a pastoral leader, or, of the members that make up the congregation during a particular time in the lifespan of a congregation."

Israel Galindo and Betty Pugh Mills, "Long-term Pastorates and Bowen Family Systems Theory"

"From experience, any progress gained in the family of origin is automatically translated into the nuclear family."

Murray Bowen in "Various Theoretical Points People Miss," Mary Bourne (ed)

"If people over time are able to differentiate more of a self in their family of origin and resolve some of the unresolved emotional attachment to the original family, then the underlying adaptiveness to stress in the nuclear family will improve."

Randall T. Frost, "The Predictability of the Family Emotional System"

"The relationship system into which a human is born, the nuclear family, is the most influential in shaping an individual's basic flexibility to adapt to life's challenges."

Patricia A. Comella, "Observing Emotional Functioning in Human Relationship Systems"

"...it probably takes at least six generations to decide whether any change that occurs in family process is a fundamental change of the recycling of symptoms."

Edwin H. Friedman, "The Birthday Party Revisited: Family Therapy and the Problem of Change" in *The Therapist's Own Family*

"In our society today, much is made of treating children as persons, human beings who have a right to be heard. But many family leaders today bend so far in the direction of consensus, in order to avoid the stigma of being authoritarian, that clarity of values and the positive, often crucial benefits of the leader's self-differentiation are almost totally missing from the system. One of the most prevalent characteristics of families with disturbed children is the absence or the involution of the relational hierarchy. While schools of family therapy have different ways of conceptualizing this condition, which may also be viewed as a political phenomenon regarding congregations, it is so diffuse among families troubled by their troubled children that its importance cannot be underestimated. What happens in any type of family system regarding leadership is paradoxical. The same interdependency that creates a need for leadership makes the followers anxious and reactive precisely when the leader is functioning best."

Edwin H. Friedman, *Generation to Generation*

"Emotional reactiveness in a family or other group that lives and works together goes from one family member to another in a chain reaction pattern. The total pattern is similar to electronic circuits in which each person is "wired" or connected by radio to all the other people with whom he has relationships. Each person then becomes a nodal point or an electronic center through which impulses pass in rapid succession or even multiple impulses at the same time.... This family systems theory postulates that all of the characteristics described under "emotional reactiveness" are all part of that part of man that he shares with lower forms of life."

Murray Bowen, *Family Therapy in Clinical Practice*

"Each generation has its own developmental tasks to work through during the various stages of the family life cycle. The more open families are across the generational boundaries, the more competent they will be in dealing with these tasks and the related stresses introduced by nodal events and unpredictable life situations."

Susan S. Edwards, "Defining Self After the Last Child Leaves Home" in *The Therapist's Own Family.*

"One family remains in contact with the parental family and remains relatively free of symptoms for life, and the level of differentiation does not change much in the next generation. The other family cuts off with the past, develops symptoms and dysfunction, and a lower level of differentiation in the succeeding generation."

Murray Bowen, *Family Therapy in Clinical Practice*

"Bowen called the capacity to maintain functioning when exposed to sustained levels of stress, or to recover functioning after a period of heightened stress, *the basic level of differentiation.* That capacity is formed in people's nuclear family in their early relationship wieth their parents (or primary caregivers), who, Bowen then postulates, have similar levels of differentiation."

Patricia A. Comella, "Observing Emotional Functioning in Human Relationship Systems"

In children who emerge with a lower basic level of differentiation "Much of the mother's thinking, worry, feeling energy goes into "giving attention" to the child, to which the child responds by "giving" and equal amount of self to mother. This is in contrast to the better differentiated mother whose giving to the child is determined by the child's need and not the mother's anxiety. The amount of mother's "giving of self" to the child constitutes a programmed "need for love" in the child that will be manifested in the child's future relationships. The amount of "need for love" tends to remain fixed for life. The amount of reciprocal "giving and receiving" in the early mother-child relationship provides the first clue of the future level of 'differentiation of self' for the child. The parent-child relationship may stay in fairly calm equilibrium until adolescence when the dependently attached child attempts to break away from parents and form peer relationships."

Murray Bowen, *Family Therapy in Clinical Practice*

"The importance of nodal events, family reunions of any type, and rites of passage cannot be underestimated. They were our species' own natural device for dealing with change and separation, the two major goals of all activity that has come to be called "therapy." They are, in fact, the original form of all therapy, and began, indeed, as family therapy."

Edwin H. Friedman, *Generation to Generation*

Bibliography

Bourne, Mary (ed)."Various Theoretical Points People Miss" in Bregman, Ona C. and White, Charles (eds). *Bringing Systems Thinking to Life: Expanding the Horizons for Bowen Family Systems Theory.* New York: Routledge. Taylor & Francis, 2011.

Bourne, Mary, (ed). "An Obstacle to 'Hearing' Bowen Theory ,"Mary Bourne (ed) " in Bregman, Ona C. and White, Charles (eds). *Bringing Systems Thinking to Life: Expanding the Horizons for Bowen Family Systems Theory.* New York: Routledge. Taylor & Francis, 2011.

Bowen, Murray. *Family Therapy in Clinical Practice.* Northvale, New Jersey: Jason Aronson, 1985.

Bregman, Ona C. and White, Charles (eds). *Bringing Systems Thinking to Life: Expanding the Horizons for Bowen Family Systems Theory.* New York: Routledge. Taylor & Francis, 2011.

Comella, Patricia A. "Observing Emotional Functioning in Human Relationship Systems" in Bregman, Ona C. and White, Charles (eds). *Bringing Systems Thinking to Life: Expanding the Horizons for Bowen Family Systems Theory.* New York: Routledge. Taylor & Francis, 2011.

Comella, Patricia et al., eds. *The Emotional Side of Organizations: Applications of Bowen Theory.* Washington, DC: Georgetown Family Center, 1996.

Friedman, Edwin H. *Generation to Generation: Family Process in Church and Synagogue.* New York: The Guilford Press, 1985.

Friedman, Edwin. *A Failure of Nerve: Leadership in the Age of the Quick Fix.* Ed. E. Beal and M. Treadwell. Seabury Books, 2007.

Galindo, Israel and Brock, Timothy, eds. Bowen Family Systems Theory in the Congregational Context. *Review & Expositor Journal.* Issue vol. 102 no. 3, (2005).

Galindo, Israel and Mills, Betty Pugh. "Long-term Pastorates and Bowen Family Systems Theory." *Review & Expositor Journal,* 2016.

Galindo, Israel. *Perspectives on Congregational Leadership.* Richmond, VA: Educational Consultants, 2009.

Galindo, Israel. *The Hidden Lives of Congregations.* Bethesda: The Alban Institute/Rowman & Littlefield, 2004.

Guerin, P. J., ed. *Family Therapy.* New York: Gardner Press, 1976.

Papero, Daniel V. *Bowen Family Systems Theory*. Boston: Allyn and Bacon, 1990.

Richardson, Ronald W. *Family Ties That Bind: A Self-Help Guide to Change Through Family of Origin Therapy*. Bellingham, Washington: International Self-Counsel Press Ltd., 1984.

Richardson, Ronald W. and Richardson, Lois A. *Birth Order and You: How Your Sex and Position in the Family Affects Your Personality and Relationships*. Bellingham, Washington: International Self-Counsel Press Ltd., 1990.

Richardson, Ronald W. *Becoming A Healthier Pastor*. Minneapolis: Augsburg Fortress Press, 2005.

Richardson, Ronald W. *Creating a Healthier Church: Family Systems Theory, Leadership, and Congregational Life*. Minneapolis: Fortress Press, 1996.

Steinke, Peter L. *Congregational Leadership in Anxious Times: Being Calm and Courageous No Matter What*. New York: Rowman & Littlefield, 2006.

Titelman, P. *Clinical Applications of Bowen family Systems Theory*. New York, Haworth Press, 1998.

Titelman, P. *Emotional Cutoff: Bowen Family Systems Theory Perspectives*. New York, Haworth Clinical Practice Press, 2003.

Titleman, P. (ed). *The Therapist's Own Family: Toward the Differentiation of Self.* New Jersey: Jason Aronson, Inc., 1987.

Priscilla J. Friesen, and Lester, Cheryl B. "A Systems View of the Training Program at the Bowen Center" in Bregman, Ona C. and White, Charles (eds). *Bringing Systems Thinking to Life: Expanding the Horizons for Bowen Family Systems Theory.* New York: Routledge. Taylor & Francis, 2011.

Made in the USA
Lexington, KY
22 November 2019